GARETH

GEORGE KLAWITTER

iUniverse LLC
Bloomington

GARETH

iUniverse books may be ordered through booksellers or by contacting:

iUniverse LLC
1663 Liberty Drive
Bloomington, IN 47403
www.iuniverse.com
1-800-Authors (1-800-288-4677)

ISBN: 978-1-4917-2099-8 (sc)
ISBN: 978-1-4917-2100-1 (e)

Printed in the United States of America.

iUniverse rev. date: 04/23/2014

Contents

Acknowledgements

The following poems appeared in *Assaracus*, ed. Bryan Borland: "His Touch As," "His Metamorphosis," "Colossus Down," "Gareth's Via Gloriosa," "Song," "At the Lake," "Gray Eyes," "The Truth about Change."

"A Letter to Gareth" appeared in *This Assignment is So Gay*, ed. Megan Vopert.

for Garrett

"Truly," he seyde, "my name is sir Gareth of Orkeney, and som men call me Bewmaynes" . . .

—*Sir Thomas Malory*

Anticipating Baptism

The last, who charmed both heart and eye,
was like a flower scarce unfolded.
It was his lot to love and die
unknown. His cheeks were shaded
with tender down, his eyes were bright,
with youthful ecstasy alight,
the violence of virgin passion
was surging in his boyish breast.

—Pushkin

An angel in white transfixed in chapel light
stands framed between a cross draped for loss
and a phallic candle leading him to cry
beyond his expectation, primed for love.

No absence in his soul, no sign of fright,
no warring demons as alleluias toss
his sprit heavenward. No vicious lie
flakes his eye, done with dawn. Above,

his wonder soars to spar with seraphim
who know his sweetness, sense his gentleness,
and shift some choirs to welcome him. Alone,

he rises, overcome. The cherubim
resume their chant, soothed. His confidence
is home at last, in peace with Rome.

Gareth

He's everything I never was: the face
of marble and the shoulders broad
as doorways, a high school football quarterback
loved by crowds and crowned by fawning mobs.

He lives in canvas, and I live in lace.
He's honesty. I'm artifice and fraud.
His happiness fills in my sullen lack
of virtue. I lecture certain truth. He nods.

He's everything I never was, and so
I love his stumbling searching for
the answers no contentment can supply.

I move in anguish he will never know
as time and distance part us more and more,
he into life and I to age and die.

Weakness

He wears his weakness like a badge
where anyone can see it, not
afraid to show its scary face
in sunshine or in springtime rain.

He finds he has a gentle brain
ripe for music. From a cage
he's loosed himself into a spot
rich with poetry, a space

of open sky, a country place.
His eyes are rarely fixed in pain
as he turns another page
of wondered world, cold or hot.

Southern wisdom's what he's got,
moving slowly pace by pace,
weathering his heart's new vane,
adjusting lovers on his stage.

The American Southwest

The desert speaks to me. In sand, in sun
I find the perfect metaphor: my soul,
desiccated, cactus-torn, lacking
food and water, clambers over rock,

avoiding lizards and the things that mock
my emptiness. I'm the only one
who wanders lost here, scratching hole to hole,
searching meaning while my brain, racking

possibilities, follows, tracking
leads, cresting dunes, taking stock
of shadows, danger. As I watch or run
from shade to shade, I sense my shifting goal

parches in the heat of day, my role
at night fighting cold. Then my lacking
meaning spindles into dust—I knock
into the god my pain and joy has won.

Rune

And though I cannot please each curious eare
With sugred Noates of heavenly Harmonie:
Yet if my love shall to thy selfe appeare,
No other Muse I will invoke but thee.
                              —Richard Barnfield

Gusty as a wind from the north
arriving in the gentle, fertile south,
ribboned to a breeze, he stands amazed
remembering his lore, arena bound,
eternal cowboy, vested, buckled, booted,
tricking rodeo god, looking west,
thinking rainbow thoughts, then riding east.

Since his reluctant darkness matters least
in earning scores garnered test to test,
myopic seem his dreams once he's rooted,
priapic, the garden faun, and sound
social butterfly, crazed and dazed,
of growing virtue's virtue hand to mouth,
noontime, midnight, sliding, gliding forth.

Escape

If you ask me which I prefer of you—
your body or your soul—I'll stand amazed,
caught up in awe, a mouse before a cat.
You bat me paw to paw under a face

anticipating lunch. What to do?
When you let me go, I wander dazed,
too weak for this and way too dumb for that,
a furry nothing loosed in time and space.

I'll wander into landscape—that's my cure—
to find in natural beauty all I need—
sunsets, geysers, redwoods, petrified trees.

No good: everything I see is torture,
you in every flower, every seed.
I'm worse than lost. You bring me to my knees.

The Ocean and the River

Plead for me, and so by thine and my labour
I am thy Creator, thou my Saviour.
                    —*John Donne*

When summer settles on the ocean, and heat
rekindles smell the land was never proud of,
a swarm of agony hovers over weeds
and dead things floating in the brine.

But the river pushes freshness beat
by beat through the delta, and the shroud of
desperation dissipates as seeds
of renovation prosper vine by vine.

You are that river bringing peace and joy
to my ancient sea of dread. I kneel
to goodness, kindness, energy. It's true—

this veneration flows from man to boy.
Rejuvenated, I wish that I could feel
about our God the way I feel about you.

Trojans and Greeks

Hector stands, the tallest of the tall,
then sits with women waiting for his cue
to skewer death, but when he meets his foe,
he runs away until the Fates say, "Stop!"

Then he faces proud Achilles: he's top
to bottom eldest prince of all,
august prince of Troy. But is he you?
A salvaged coward, soft, for all we know.

Paris next. As love would have it so,
a gorgeous boy with hair a wanton mop,
but Menelaus rises, makes him bawl.
With Aphrodite's helpful misty dew

he's back to sleepy Helen. As the rue
drops on her carpet, he watches anger grow.
So are you this disheveled boy-toy fop,
a prissy archer bracing for a fall?

And Dolon, captured as he tries to crawl
among the Greeks, well-intentioned (few
would disagree)—he stumbles over row
on row of sleeping soldiers when a pop

makes him pause. His heart begins to drop.
Odysseus appears in the pall
of darkness, grabs him, ascertains the hue
of fear. Is Dolon's angst yours? No.

Where are you on the battlefield? A crow
above the din looks down, as it can hop
limb to limb, wall to broken wall,
searching for your face more red than blue.

Suddenly it senses, near a crew
of Myrmidons, a singer. Even though
rank horror screams, you strum your poem, a sop
of beauty bloodied there where trumpets call.

Hopeless

I've discovered something you can't do
despite your wiliness, your craft and art—
despite the strength I feel in your arms,
you just can't rip your image from my heart.

Try to excavate what I have of you
fissured in my tissue, every part
guarded tight against your Texan charm,
your appetite for wonder painful, smart.

You're rooted in the contours of my flesh.
Give up! No master plan will help you win
your freedom as you grovel, cry, and sue.

Boa constrictor, tightening a fresh
reminder tense, spin by daily spin,
I want to start eternity with you.

The Question

The secrete thoughtes imparted with such trust,
The wanton talke, the divers change of play,
The frenship sworne, eche promise kept so just,
Wherwith we past the winter nightes away.
            —Henry Howard, Earl of Surrey

Why should I call it anything but love?
"Friendship" is inadequate—the word
implies that distance makes small difference
when bodies cleave and souls are pulled apart.

He leaves, I ache. He takes away my heart.
I wonder at the residue above
my mind. With every platitude I've heard
I shake, an ugly surge of emptiness.

As he discovers the softer side of him
and leaves the raucous clank of bone on bone,
in music all the poetry that grows
inside will undermine his antic fears.

When a soul invades a soul, it hears
new melodies, new harmonies, that few
can hear. "I love him" is my newest song.
Should I tell him? He already knows.

July, 2011, Chicago

If I thought a thousand miles would ease
the ache of weekly separation, I
was wrong. The blowing beeches scream your name,
and the Norway maple in the corner

of the yard shapes its darkness as it sees
my dismal loss of you. Then the sky
smeared with rainclouds makes the dreary frame
of daylight snake the path the lilacs border,

while the summer robins frolic gamely
hunting this and that in the sullen grass.
These are the images that carry thoughts
of you so distant I can't tell what's true.

But then the sun redeems the garden, mainly
columbine and yarrow. All things pass—
shoulds and woulds, maybes, even oughts—
today five times I didn't think of you.

The Time for Answers

You think you're alone. The darkness swims
across your mind and grips your body tight,
a python squeezing for an easy kill
as you grab the final loss of light.

I have a darkness too. It works on whims.
It strikes with fangs and supernatural night
inside a murky cave. No wish or will
can counteract its misdefining bite.

You're not alone. The morning star
that smiles alike on angels and on vipers
heralds the cleansing comfort of the sun
whether you want it to or not. It ripens

in my darkest flowers. Where you are
it shines. Our serpents eat each other, snipers,
Joy, Unjoy, catching us. We are as one
in resurrection, bodies linked by hyphens.

Transfer: The Wren and the Cat

Let's say you've bought a bird, a wren,
and put him in a gaily painted cage
near a window where the sunshine warms
him, coaxing him to sing his nicest song.

But he doesn't sing. He pines and pouts, and when
you read him poetry, page after page,
he finds his mirror, ignores your smiles and storms,
enjoys his sweet reflection. Before long

you lose your interest in everything,
then turn and see the cat, sleek and blond,
lazing by the open fireplace,
indolent, tail swinging wide.

You remember how his purring used to sing
across the Texas twilight, demimonde.
You catch his eye and cross the empty space,
rub his back, then settle down side by side.

An Angel Comes to Town

I knew an angel once. A windy gust,
he blew across my doorway, found a seat
and sat seraphically munching poetry
to my delight. I never saw him cry

but once, and that because he said he must.
Usually he laughed, a deep repeat
from somewhere in his soul, the agony
of ecstasy, the sense of do or die.

Now he's off with cherubim somewhere.
Don't ask me how he handles life. I wish
I knew. He's so deliberate I sense

his mind revolves on wheels. Inside there
the powers and virtues poise and bait and fish
while I can only wonder what his beauty meant.

Birds at Play

My love is of a birth as rare
As 'tis for object strange and high.
It was begotten by despair
Upon impossibility.
                    —Andrew Marvell

I don't know why I'm writing poems to you
except the process takes the pressure
off my tethered soul. It's not that words
will open up your heart to what I say:

you have your own agenda, old or new.
I have mine, open to your censure
or your praise, and so I write of birds,
caged or wild, active night and day.

Here's another nightingale singing
for his life, dying for the moon,
happy for the tiniest of chances,

and there you are, to stares or glances
indifferent alike, in all you do
a tense regality, an eagle bringing

order, peace, and joy. If I may
presume to catch your beauty now in words
that effervesce every time I mention
you, I will create new ways to true

my sight, yet the phrases slip out day
by day as you soar away, hordes
of words inadequate to the pleasure
come of seeing you as words won't do.

Two Medics

I sing to you even when no words
appear, my song a voiceless song of awe
too deep for phrase or even syllable:

you there, me here, and everything I saw
in you between, both link and loving gulf,
impassable, surpassable, a wonder

fit for revelations of the self,
yourself, myself, nothing lost or missed,
mindless, mindful, a paradox of tears

and laughter, bantered for a breathless kiss
or not, as the airy games filter
back and forth like a shuttlecock,

merciless in mercy, heart-spilled,
growing nightly, dying daily, inter-
rupted by the suture of our souls.

Anatomy

Long ago the wisest Roman didn't think it stupid
to play horse-back riding with the boys.
                    —Thomas Watson, Amyntas

Fifty years is not so long a time
I'd take to understand the gentle quiet
of your soul, but what about the flash
that vigor spins inside your fiery eyes?

I guess I'll use eternity, for by it
you can be corralled, and thus the dash
that interrupts your virtue, nature's prize,
will settle to a softness, sweet, sublime.

But when I feel your body, a sudden rash
subdues my skin: how can I match the size
your shadow throws when conscience whispers "crime"
and muscle struggles with your strength and beauty?

I'll need a new eternity that dies
each day you come to build from stone and slime
our other self devoid of game and duty—
just you and me and it abrupt, unasked.

The Workshop

I've smashed all the statues in my studio
except the one of you. That one I'll keep.
Not that you're hard and can't be ever broken.
No, you're delicate, like porcelain.

Somewhere in my heart, in a fissure deep
with manly prayer, where love and peace are spoken,
you were chiseled hard and masculine.
Then in the darkness sweet hands soothed your mood.

So now transported, a fine-arts token,
to live you've galvanized a feminine
revision to your soul and made it food
for angels, those who creep into your sleep.

From the shards in my shop of course I can
create another man to rival you,
but I won't. It is enough to weep
your beauty daily, my life reawoken.

Wonders

You say you've seen a rabbit kill a snake,
the sun rise bloody in a jungle rot
of green and brown, a camel filter
through a doorway narrow as a slice

of sunshine, forest morel mushrooms slake
their thirst on a dinosaur not
ten minutes dead, an honest realtor,
a beauty queen with a head full of lice.

These wonders, yes, are wonders, but your eye
has yet to see a marvel kings would pay
a prince's ransom to behold, a thing

more marvelous than when or where or why
a choir of devils and angels merged can say
"Witness, a straight man and a gay man sing."

Winnowing the Chaff

When I'm done admiring every inch of you,
what will I do? Move on to other game?
Take my bow, move back into the forest
where cougars purr, toucans whistle in the trees?

There set my snare, try to forget your name?
Wait until a beast attacks and gore is
running down my chest as golden bees
and wild ants gather for the view?

I can't just sit around for fate. More's
the shame I've let strength or beauty seize
initiative letting the likes of who
falls in my heart orchestrate my shame.

No, I'd better hunt my own, the he's
that populate my dreams, down to a few,
then pare my choice to one alone to blame
as quarry, one—it's you, my lord of lords.

What Love Creates

At some point I will go or you will go,
but the parting will be gentle, like
lips about to speak or kiss, and then
our hearts will understand the joy

we nurtured through the summer when roses grow
as thoughts, simple, direct, and pure, a spike
of love and thorn side by side. So when
the separation comes, it's man from boy.

You knew it when we touched that things untouch,
that doors once locked unlock, that vistas new
and rich appear where darkness made us one.

You're you—I'm me—and in between there's such
a being love created, neither I nor you
can stop our wonder as it reaches for the sun.

After the Storm

The thing is he's infinitely patient
waiting in his cool tabernacle
with the candles blinking softly
like bubbles in a Yellowstone mud flat.

He knows you'll turn and run
to other colors, forgetting beige
for amethyst and emerald,
letting a sun lure you into light.

The circle turns. I'm left
with him, and he understands,
as he always does, I'd return
empty-handed, sore, and hard.

His calm will soften me.
I'll listen for his whisper,
and when it comes, I'll bend my neck
and know he's won again.

The Cat

I have a cat. Full of hair.
Soft eyes. A smile to fight for.
Cheshire, he disappears at will,
independent as Satan.

He responds to love, his downfall,
so I protect him from strangers
eager to take him in for petting,
to see themselves reflected in his iris.

He trusts his instinct,
but a Tarot card would better
his nonchalance about connections.
I worry about him, vulnerable.

How do I keep him out of alleys?
Away from vultures out for his heart?
An open bowl of lobster bisque
can only go so far.

After that it's just hope,
dumb hope, he'll find
his way back here, scratched
and scented, wiser for his falls.

He answers to no name
so I coo "Absolom"
and sometimes "Hadrian."
If he understands, I never know.

He listens when I read him poetry,
his body numb with pleasure,
rigid as a rib of celery
primed for ecstasy.

Inscrutable as a furry mountain,
he'll take my time of fifty years.
Then I'll say with confidence,
"I know him, soul and body."

Love without Sex

O Thou, my lovely boy, who in thy power
Dost hold Time's fickle glass, his sickle hour,
Who hast by waning grown, and therein show'st
Thy lover's withering as thy sweet self grow'st…
                    —William Shakespeare

You drive me into God where I flounder
like a beached whale, broken-finned,
rudderless, knowing there is cause
but unsure of why as the sun,

morning-born, pitiless, rounder
than the truth, dries my vulgar skin,
sinks my tragic eyes into a pause
demanding ministry from all or none.

Then the hammer in my brain for fun
strikes the witching juice to swirl from jaws
to nether parts of me where the sin
of missing you fuses into sound or

silence, the difference pounding one
against the other, making virtue raw
from rubbing thoughts of you in the din
of light throbbing, ecstasy found at last.

Fishing

When you went fishing, you knew you'd pull me in,
sitting yourself weekly in my class
with pen and line, pretending you didn't care
if I were there or not, waiting, waiting,

until I grabbed the hook. You knew my sin
of weakness for your strength and the flash
of beauty in your face. You set your snare
to catch me breathless sooner or later.

When I went fishing, I knew I'd pull you in.
I baited my hook with poetry and waited
in the shallows of your fretful brain
so when you were distracted you would strike.

I knew the day I saw you I would win,
recording to the second when I stated
"you're mine" and yanked the line until the strain
of wonder hooked your soul, wrong or right.

Then there's the master fisherman who wanted
us to meet. He stirred the waters with
his ancient hand until we swirled into
the eddy of his love in fear and awe.

You swam to me, I swam to you, undaunted
by the master's hook, his watery wish
we intertwine our destinies: men who,
caught into each other, loved what they saw.

That Dumb Fuck

It happens every fifteen years—
you meet a man who knocks you off your feet.
Everything he does is godly.
Every breath you breathe of his is sweet.

Auden had his Christopher,
and Housman, Moses Jackson.
Achilles had Patroclus.
Each Angle had his Saxon.

So you finally find a friendly man
who nicely fits into your crowded life.
You sing him songs until one day
he cuts your heart up with his Bowie knife.

Boo-hoo, boo-hoo, how sad for you—
you eat a poisoned apple,
then spit it out and scream and shout,
and run into the chapel.

There in the cool of candlelight
one waits for you. You need no fate or luck.
You genuflect, sit in a pew,
facing the tabernacle and its dumb fuck.

You wait for him, he waits for you.
The game is slow and hot.
He knew you'd come—you always do—
whether he needs you or not.

So you've been dumped by another man
and rather than throw yourself before a truck,
you've thrown yourself in front of God
who always takes you back, the stupid fuck.

The Sparrow and His Keeper

Dream not of other worlds, what creatures there
Live, in what state, condition, or degree,
Contented that thus far hath been revealed
Not of earth only but of highest Heaven.
                    —John Milton, *Paradise Lost*

If he ever wondered how it is
that I can love him man to man, he never
raised the question, simply letting nature
be what nature is, better or worse.

Where others find my love unfair or cruel,
he lets it wing its way uncaged. He knows
I'm tethered to his heart, can't really fly
much farther than his thought—or rather mine.

Somehow I feel he's greater than a god
because he works on instinct, letting sense
impel him, not omniscience, so the gamble
I'll always be there always keeps him here,

inside my aging heart, where minutes turn
to years and centuries to eons, ever
steadfast, knowing gods can never do
what we do—hope eternity will last.

In August Heat

The summer is over, and my cat is gone.
His favorite chair sits empty while the thrill
of seeing him ebbs into an ache
of red and purple laced with black and gray.

The Texas sun hangs heavy in a haze
of memory while the drought dusts through
my hope of hearing him purring weekly
at the door gentled by my love.

But I can look around my life, above
the folds of recollection where he meekly
prowls awaiting anxiously a new
endorsement via poetry, amazed

my love endures. He understands it may
extend into eternity and take
its time maturing. I know it will.
I also know I'll never stop my songs.

The Truth will Out

If there are as many minds as there are heads,
then there are as many kinds of love as there are hearts.
—Leo Tolstoy, trans. Andrea Rossing

You told me you were straight, and I believed you.
Every time you raised the issue, I
said yes, yes, you're certainly not queer—
as normal as a hetero can be.

But each night that you sighed as I relieved you,
I wondered if the labels we live by
are firm or liquid. Evenings when you're near
to climax a man's the only thing I see.

Call yourself whatever, just love me
and let the world go hang in hate or fear.
I live for you, and I would even die

if you ever needed me to die. I'm he
who follows you in hope from there to here,
touched enough to make us laugh or cry.

The Lesson

If he learns anything from me
I hope it's love, the feeling and the sense
of living for another, realizing
the fragility of joy is worth the pain.

The distances that separate can be
measured in emotions and the dense
arteries of liquid surge capsizing
obstacles society maintains.

I love him over mountains of regret
and deserts laced with scorpions of rules.
I love him when the sun says I should not

because the evening with its moon will let
me love him. Acrobats and fools
accept me as I juggle him and God.

Believe Me

You have sugared my groin.
> —*Jack Spicer*

I never realized
what you did to me
until I realized

you have sugared my groin.

Now I will never cry
except in happiness
because I realize

you have sugared my groin.

Water or Air

All love is likely to be illicit.
                          —Muriel Rukeyser

The soul's a funny thing—
it finds a proper love,
then dismisses other suitors
knowing one's enough.

When you slid into my life,
my soul blinked once or twice,
then cauterized its former hurts,
no longer rolled the dice.

You swim in my regard,
blow bubbles like a fish,
lounge around aquarium-bound,
a captive to my wish.

I know that you could flee
if the trout inside you tried
to escape the ocean of my soul—
no matter if I'd died.

My task's a simple one—
I have to sing enough
to keep you in your water cage,
a prisoner of my love.

The Lie Exposed

I lied when I said
on nightmare days all I need
is to think of you and happiness
swells its way into my soul.

Today in the ashes of hell
I summoned you
as the ugly swirls
of desperation deafened me.

I thrashed in pitch and tar
waiting for the softening lave
of water you could bring.
Nothing came but dark over dark.

I could go into the garden
to be distracted by frond and thorn,
but sunlight would heighten
the passion of your loss.

The only remedy is you,
not the thought of you,
not memory or fantasy,
but only you. Please come back.

Reality

My cat is coming back.
He'll arch his back and purr
as he comes in the front door
and heads to his favorite chair.

It's my favorite chair too,
but he doesn't care
since he commandeers it as easily
as he's commandeered my life.

If he's overwhelmed by my love,
he never lets me know.
He tolerates my petting
and snoozes most of the time.

I don't know what he makes
of my overbearing love.
Sometimes I think he returns
just for the food and attention.

Just like a cat! So regal!
Descended as they like to think
from an ancient line of kings
and so they deserve what they deserve.

I don't care. He's here.
Sometimes I think I'm fascinated
only by the love I have
for him, not him himself.

And so we play our little games.
He curls up in happiness
while I go about my nervous life
trying to assess the situation.

My Cat in the Future

Someday my cat
won't be pretty any more.
Will I still love him?

His skin will wrinkle
like creases in day-old pies
or faces on English bulldogs.

His hair will hang
in scraggly patches
here and there gone gray.

His eyes won't burn
in agony or loss
as they once did.

He'll have the energy
of a garden slug
and sleep most of the day.

Wait! I'm forgetting
he smokes. He smokes!
He'll be dead by thirty-three.

The coal tar in his lungs
will spread slowly
to his pretty soul,

and all his joys
will dessicate,
crumble with his bones.

Then I'll go to his grave
to weep and leave a poem
under a pebble on his stone.

And I'll smoke for him
and flick the ashes on him
just the way he liked it.

It's the least I can do
for the cat I loved
then, now, and beyond.

Despair

My cat will never come back.
He's found a new home where
they've given him a hole
to pour in all his deep anxieties.

It's a little tight, but
that's the way he likes it—
snug and humid, darkened
for his wild pleasure.

I don't know what I miss
the most—his ample hair,
his quiet quaint anticipation
of the evening's fare,

his thickened muscle tightened
for the kill, his manly sense
of duty once the deed is done,
fulfillment rushing through his veins.

Maybe it's just his presence,
never knowing what he'll think
or how he'll move, every gesture
sweet to me, appreciated, loved.

The house is here, everything
exactly how he left it,
a shrine now to his absence
in the growing darkness of my heart.

Always Feline

I close my eyes, and he comes
soft and delicate, like summer pebbles
softened by a summer rain,

but with winter in his face,
and in his eyes the tortured hint
of snow and ice.

I wish he were eternal spring,
but his walk is ever movement
to a seasoned mind of change.

Like humankind, his autumn,
his most careful phase,
maneuvers sadly through my heart.

The Sweet Return

My cat may be back.
At least I think he's back.
The neighborhood is vastly quiet
as if anticipating a great man.

The heat sequestered us for months,
tight against our own emotions,
but the joy of seeing him
releases in the garden something grand.

The Lady Baltimore hibiscus heightens
all her strengths for him
to push some final pink
into the warm September gauze.

The Texas yellow-bells are shouting
to the sun "he's back"
and straining for the roof
they've always envied more or less.

The cacti, prim in their terra cotta,
grin into the arching sun of autumn
knowing he'll be scratching back,
ready for their thorns and thrills.

I myself stare at the window
waiting for his sweet return,
no questions, only answers,
swimming in the final summer strains.

The Wheel

I didn't think he'd dump me quite this soon.
The summer reveries that shredded love
between our aching souls, mine more than his
apparently, evaporated as

the August heat retreated for the moon
September brings to cool us from above
whatever passion twinned our hearts and is
one sweet reminder that his rainbow has

endured if he has not. I cater whims
among the young who garden in my soul
and harvest what they need, then smile and leave.

My consolation is the clutch of hims
who populate my brain. Never a hole
that can't be filled, a boy's love water in a sieve.

Going Off

Afraid of love he stepped around it like
the cat he is, ginger in his hair
and in his heart. I couldn't tell him, "Look,
the pain is worth the effort." No, he'd rather

walk alone than walk with me, the spike
of sun reflecting off his back, no care
for friendship by the heart or by the book.
It makes a weasel pause to gauge the matter.

We're born for aches like separation.
A pet curls up and dies without so much
as nuzzling one last time, vacant as

a lone star blinking, or the vindication
absence brings to him who worked for such,
the prince of cats, wandering as he has.

The Ritual

In forty-eight hours
my cat'll be back.
He'll sit here for hours
expecting a snack.

I'll feed him iambics
and wait for his verse.
I'll pet him and fete him.
Life could be worse.

The dry spells between,
when he isn't here,
pass slowly and blandly,
each hour a year.

But then he shows up.
The day has a smile.
I pace him to heaven
mile after mile.

But I know he'll leave.
The sun will recede
except when I conjure—
he'll come when I need.

Sunset

Blinded by the orange and pink
of an autumn sunset,
I will suffer this, I think,
as my final fling with beauty,
knowing you will ride away
with the seeds of my love
accepted in your mind and heart.

The sunset melts into the night
as evening creatures excavate
the garden roots and soil,
but the darkness is a cover
for the thoughts I've planted
in your greening soul
to resurrect spring after spring.

Dark and Light

I'm not ashamed to admit that my unfortunate Amyntas
is humiliated, poor, and sick, not hoping for his own health
but for his own happy death.
            —Thomas Watson, Amyntas

When a month escapes into a year
without my seeing you, and my eyes
deaden into lumps of lead unfocussed
in the gray of another day

without you, I can manage to live here,
a garden stone among the garden lies,
hoping for a tulip spring and crocus
when you return singing throughout May.

Without the hope of seeing you again
I'm dead. Without the faith of growing
in your sight, I'm just a vegetable

of memories and garden wit. Pretend
that you need me, and then in growing
near me love will blossom unregrettable.

The Wanton Summer

The passion vine
has spilled its thrill
onto the sidewalk.

I'll let it go strangling
the sego palm, muffling
the bird of paradise,

blocking the cactus
from its beloved
ever-beaming light.

Everywhere I look
the purple-gold
dominates my garden.

How long can you resist?

Cat and Mouse

I thought I was a weasel,
but I'm not. I'm a mouse.
You bat me with your fuzzy paws
one pat after another until
I'm dizzy in the summer heat.

You play with me back and forth
while I look up, dazed
and captivated, waiting for
the kill which never comes
because it never will.

I'm caught in the ecstasy
of your uncertain power
and could not escape
even if I wanted to—
which I don't.

Colors

*The spirit that is powerful and clear in free repose
is the same spirit as in passionate desire.*
                              —Vladimir Solofyov

When morning light reminds me I'm alone,
colors arch across my waking brain.
There's golden for the haystack of your beard
and fawn-tipped gray the fancy of your eyes.

Your skin is marble, and the ancient tone
cerise seeps gently from your heart to stain
my thoughts. Whatever leopards I had feared
for loving you dissolve to no surprise.

Your versicolor soul excites my soul.
Your palette daubed with green and royal blue
besmears my canvas, a kaleidoscope

of changing hues and shapes, your artist role
to paint me over, brush the old to new
with crimson faith and rich magenta hope.

Fatal Abstraction

Once every fifteen years I fall off a cliff
in a descent that's swift, a matter of months,
no time to notice the mountain goats and sheep
that line the crevices munching grass.

If I could even notice the time to pass
in blips I would, but I can't—it's as if
I'm so obsessed with sensation, become a dunce
to reality, I may as well be asleep.

But that nirvana as it would slowly creep
across my drowsy eyes, a shark that has
to swim or die, might slice open a rift
between us. I won't allow it, not once

I knew the moss and lichens where he hunts
me at the bottom would cushion us deep
and deeper when he plunges me to lapse
in ecstasy while in his love I drift.

On Vacation

My cat is out there
somewhere
looking for a pussy.

After he's done
he sleeps
next to a tree

letting a slice
of sunlight
dance in his brown hair.

In the First Garden

That, as an harpe obeieth to the hand
and maketh it soune after his fyngerynge,
right so mowe ye oute of myn herte bringe
swich vois, right as you lyst, to laughe or pleyne.
                    —*Chaucer, LCW*

There where we knew nothing
but perfection in each other,
where the sun rose warm
on our tender flesh
and night brought cool dark
to refresh our dreams in love,

where you turned to me above
the softened violets as something
rustled gently in the grass, a bother
to neither of us, never in storm,
no conflict, nothing but the best
of goodness and the spark

of love, quiet in our Eden park,
among the fern, the owl, the dove,
the wren, the hummingbird, anything
to soothe our comfort in another
swath of touch, no fright, alarm,
or sense of sin, no lack, lest

our lovingness corrupt, no test
or interdict, everywhere the mark
we knew in you, in me, tough
through wonder in our wondering
why your beauty never faded to smother
what you created hour by hour, no harm

to bruise our love as we charmed
our souls to fumble and then rest
our bodies one on one, a lark
sufficient and dew enough
to herald day, dethundering
our passion thick, as brother

to brother, man to man, we mothered
each other, fathered our gaze, farmed
our innocence in that nest
of love, of willow and cinnamon bark,
roses, hyacinth, to hover
soul in soul, resexing everything.

Gray Eyes

Quiet over steel, gray eyes focus
from his soul out into a light
murky with the smoke that night
mists from the evening's hocus-pocus.

Useless to resist the power of his eyes
when they fix you with a stare
meant to kill, then eat, over glare
from iris glinting off the starry skies.

No message from the touch of quiet paws
as he firms, intent for a strike
lightning-swift, jagged, nothing like
the velvet rationale of laws.

Once you're meshed between his teeth,
accept new life his way through his flesh,
turgid, understood he's master, the guess
of "no" absorbed to "yes" above, beneath.

Life Plods On

Shakespeare did not have cum shots.
                    —*Eating Out 4: Drama Camp*

It's possible to live
without him. Blood
continues to move

capillary to capillary,
the heart beating
somewhat on time.

Birds continue to sing,
a little off-key,
out there in some tree.

The last time I looked
the hibiscus in the garden
was still in bloom,

not near as vibrant,
of course, as the passion vine
spilling purple to the grass.

The sun is where
it's supposed to be
I guess, and the moon

hangs as lonely as ever,
maybe more lonely,
in the torrid night.

But it's life inside,
outside, and in between,
where my mechanical mind

conjures him any time
I need a fix,
a solitary, throbbing fix.

Return from Separation

With every push of stem and cough of bark,
our springtime grows inside my crippled heart,
and rain begins to ease the winter drought
as dirt absorbs the hesitating drops.

Nothing comes of fervor. The tin mind stops
to wonder at the iris in the dark
of February Texas-style. My part
subsides to ticking through an acting bout:

I'm here—you're there. The miles in between
fill up with oleander, myrtle, wispy grass.
The seasons are diversions. From above

the scents of new-born things, we grope unseen
each other in the dark. Our angels pass.
We are who we are, and we love whom we love.

Your Fate and Mine

Vissi d'arte, vissi d'amore.
>   —*Puccini, Tosca*

Do you really think that when I die
I'll be leaving you? Look closely
when they close the lid on my box
and worms begin their magic work

of transformation—I'll filter out
into the flowered room and find my way
into your tears, push every ounce of football
to the sidelines and resurrect myself

in you, just as I've done in every poem
I've wedged into your happy Texas heart.
You needn't fear I've gone, not even for
the moment of a moment. Every time

you look into your soul I'll wrinkle in
your life again, a morph of dreams and sweat
and every word you spoon into a poem.
I gave myself to you a year ago.

Moving On

Like a gust he spun into my life,
and I'm afraid that like a gust he'll leave.
The day will darken to a close, and crows
will crowd the blackened limbs of evening oaks.

I'm packing, so there's little time to grieve
about the life we could have lived. I suppose
the festering will heal with time and jokes,
forgetting pain ensues once the knife

has cut where it will cut. The Texas sun
will rise again on bluebonnets, the pink
of springtime wine cups will recreate the lawn
in cheap pastel. Somehow verbena will

enhance the pastures purple, and I think
the future may survive because of dawn,
that balm for aching hearts, mine, his, until
we merge again eternal, ever one.

As Time Passes

My soul has blended with yours
so now I am two men.

I used to like myself, a sullen desert,
but now I much prefer you,

the preppy colt from a dusty town
who scares the world with vitality.

Before I merged with you I caught life
on the fly, facing winds of uncertain gust,

healing barely after fights with depression,
hoping there be hope around the bend.

Now I wait to see in your gray eyes
the meaning of my meaning, and I rest

quiet in your beauty, man in man,
alone at last with peace a possibility.

Gareth's Via Gloriosa

With fingers as delicate as sparrow legs
he writes a poem about the crucified
one, a poem in halves, a brutal half
of tortured limbs, a garish half
of polished abs and golden sinews.

Where he got his double Jesus
I can guess: the endless afternoons
of football flesh on flesh in Texas heat
seared the broken bones into his lines,
along with sweat and blood and fear,

but the gentle force of love he's tamed
by sweet intelligence has monitored
iambics into Christ-the-gymnast
climbing on the iron bars intent
to gentle muscle into bulging rapture.

And then he moves, a force of grace,
a wonder in the crowd of faces turned
when he walks by or speaks a piece,
and I'm among them, jostled to the front
as the dense parade goes by:

Simon next to me stunned now
by his fifteen minutes in the sun
struggling under wood, Veronica
across the street clutching a bloody rag
she'll hoist for visitors on weekends,

a gaggle of weeping women lost
in wonder at the fusion of his miracles
with daily needs to bathe and exercise,
and lonesome John who watches thunderstruck,
sinking by the hour into dreams of sex,

all because the massive one accepted
death by footsteps heading to a tree
where the father waits nails at hand
to take him at his sacrificial best
and pin him, softened athlete, to the cross.

Passion

Some men a forward motion love,
But I by backward steps would move,
And when this dust falls to the urn
In that state I came return.
                        —*Henry Vaughan*

You think I'm going to say "good-by" today.
You think my farewell is coming this afternoon.
Your problem is you don't know passion.

Yes, you could break me in two with
your football strength, break me into
pieces for the scrap heap of memory.

But I can snap your soul with poetry,
the crisp of metaphor wrenching soul in two,
leaving you gasping in the dust of my living room.

Just try your arms along my spine.
You're no match for my similes,
my images ranked in pentameter.

I'd knock you into tears even as I crawl
from your punches to my face and chest.
I'll beat you into beauty any day. Try me.

You are my last bright chance
to be what I never was—
physical, athletic, divine.

When Parting Comes

Lo, I confess, I am thy captive I,
And hold my conquered hands for thee to tie.
What need'st thou war? I sue to thee for grace.
With arms to conquer armless men is base.
          —Ovid, Elegy 2, trans. Marlowe

What will I say when it's time to say good-by?
Should I lie and say it's not good-by
but only Auf Wiedersehen or Via con Dios
or something like Aloha containing both
coming and going, a frozen now and never?

I could say nothing but just stare,
let you puzzle out the message from my eyes,
figure out the ecstasy and agony
spun from remorse and happiness
mixing in a jumble of emotion.

There's always denial—I'm not going,
you're not staying. And there's the metaphorical
I'm-in-you and you're-in-me so any split's
impossible, even as my heart is splitting
and my mind is reeling into future mode.

The truth is I don't know what to say.
Any words will fumble in the end zone,
the game gone into overtime,
the refs frustrated, and our fans
bewildered why we're even separating.

There's memory, already percolating
into overdrive, reliving summer bliss
and autumn folly, winter resurrection
and springtime revelations. But reminiscence
falters, a second best at best.

So we're back to truth, where love depends
on love's growing every day by touch,
and touch by distance isn't really touch—
it's all pretend as the heart shatters
into paper flakes dropping piece by piece.

I love you wildly or not at all.
The angels know it since they tended it.
Your love for me is evident
so our separation's reckless, purposeless,
a mystery too secret to relock,

no substitution for your athletic strength,
your loyalty and diligence, your flaws,
your chasms and your mountaintops,
the part of you I've never traveled
except in dreams honeycombed with touch.

The truth is I can't say how life will be
without you because I can't imagine life
without you, the darkness imminent and ominous,
the future one vast plain of cloud and rain,
our separation unbelievable yet real.

Song

Run away now, hetero boy,
run as fast as you can
because if you stop running, boy,
you'll be caught by the homo-man.

Yes, he has nails of silver steel
and lives in a ginger box.
He collects little boys just like you
and eats their flabby cocks.

Run and hide in a Christmas tree—
put tinsel in your hair
and ornaments where your balls used to be.
He'll never find you there.

Or maybe he will! Then he'll grab you
with all your chocolaty fears.
He'll spoon you golden butterscotch
and dry your lemony tears.

He'll hang you up in a wicker bag
like the Sybil of Cumae,
and rain or shine you'll fatten for him
on bon-bons and crème brulée.

There you'll swing to his every whim
aside the bong-bong tree.
He'll feed you nuts in formaldehyde
until you're as plump as he.

Then he'll pinch your pretty bottom
and tongue along your ribs,
and you can sing whatever you want,
but remember that you are his.

He'll sharpen his knife and ping his fork
along your pearly teeth,
then upend you for a final lick
and tickle you underneath.

You'll squirm for a bit and whimper too
at the sound of the dinner gong,
and then he'll suck your delectable toes
and chant the blessing song.

You'll soon relax into the feast
with gravy on your chest.
There's no place to hide when you're inside
as the only succulent guest.

He'll sigh a bit as he carves your knees
and reaches for hot sauce.
You're not well done, only medium,
but luscious enough for the boss.

So heed my call to get out of town
or you'll wish like hell you did
because homo-man likes hetero boys
like you, you lucky kid.

The Kiss

If I kissed you I could taste the poison,
the slow sad death that's killing you
I know—it killed my father years ago
before you screamed your first boy breath, the air

waiting for your gasp, your clutch at new
life tense with your antiseptic soul
and nurses white on white. Life was there
and precious, something to be loved, like reason

itself. But now it walks away befouled
by nicotine and cancers nipping where
your beauty used to be, in every season
your scent beginning melancholy, blue.

So are you too far gone to dare or scare?
Can you resist the black-tar ghost, be chosen
for redemption by a kiss? My loves are few—
come back to health, my Texas man, be whole.

Those Tuesday Summer Evenings

You came to me a porcupine
of grisly sweat and guilt
for crimes you thought immense
and I thought insignificant

except that they were mountains
in the way of journey
to the seam of self-acceptance,
the reach of heaven.

You snuggled your needles
into my aging heart and said
you needed to learn self-discipline,
wanted to learn self-discipline,

So you worked your quills
every Tuesday for an hour or two
into poetry, yours, mine, and that
of our poet du jour, crabbed or raw.

How quaint to come to me for
discipline! But I ruffled
your underbelly, soft as dew,
into my runagate mind

where it waxed daily into god
and flexed its Adonis deep
into the fissures of a heart gone stone
from decades of remorse and dread.

Then each quill you barbed quivering
into my shivering body, bled my cold
incompetence, morphed me
human drop by bloody drop.

I reveled in your animal gaze,
poured my love into a hundred poems
designed to phrase my art
to your unsuspecting heart.

So much for self-discipline!
How can you learn from superfluous?
Each time you edged your bristles home
I knew conversion worked, but not my way.

Each time you waddled away
I'd fling my flaccid imagination
to the stars, words tumbling
to the sheets of waiting white.

Anyway, self-discipline is over-rated,
better in talk than practice.
To hell with it, I told myself—
my porcupine needs something better.

And so your discipline found me.
I was changed. Gradually my pores
grew baby quills, and I could stab
my way to contact just like you.

You taught me touch, each barb
of touch folded to caress,
and life moved into life,
contact by contact, touch by touch.

Our Game

I love a ghost. It may be ever so
since I throw my arms into the air
anticipating the crush of his arms
when all my bones would splinter, my blood
would rush into my eyes, my cock
ever alert for his gesture and his touch.

Then my soul would race to overtime
as the referees conferred about
the need for give and take in the art
of sport, the necessity of knowing when
to pass and when to rush, to grab and hold,
or let the sweet release of joy relax

the joints and tumble into ecstasy,
the body left to slacken into ease,
the mind relieved of care, uncare, and pain,
while all the juice of love seeped where it would
and no one minded because the players fell
into each others' arms and danced their dance.

That was all I lived for when you were there,
so now I recreate those happy days
with eyes half closed. The moments pass.
I fumble in the dark waiting for your yes,
your no, your strength tightened into dream,
everything focused on the cream of love.

Sea-Chanty

My hetero man's
   a real man—
he fucks the girls
   whenever he can.

He throws them up
   against a tree—
he fingers their ass
   and kisses their knee.

They squirm a bit—
   he doesn't care.
He slaps their face
   and rips their hair.

He claims he's only
   a hetero man,
but I know better,
   his biggest fan.

Yes, my hetero man's
   a real man—
he fucks the girls
   whenever he can.

But in his mind
   against that tree
it's never a girl—
   it's always "me."

At the Lake

There where the water reaches land
stood a man your height, your weight, your age,
fishing. He wore a baseball cap backwards.
The evening sun glinted off his face.

No noise desecrated the holy place
as he turned and shifted in the sand
to look at me, intruder on his stage.
The scene was brief, intense, and slightly awkward,

as if he were the prey and I the stalker,
he the fish and I inside his space,
the fisher rumpling the water, reeling and
waiting for this book to turn a page,

move on, he the novice, I the sage,
my eye catching you in him, but darkly.
I passed by, he fished, our hearts in a race
to fuse, now I the boy and you the man.

His Touch As

sudden as a flash of lightning,
deliberate as piano keys,

common as a denominator,
unusual as a budding phoenix,

subtle as the kiss of a python,
open as a festive Torah,

native as a Texas bluebonnet,
foreign as an alpine edelweiss,

ancient as a Roman coin,
new as a crying baby,

soft as a marmoset,
prickly as a barrel cactus,

dulcet as a summer oboe,
acrid as an unripe persimmon,

gentle as a feathered cherub,
harsh as a winter wind,

lovely as a monarch butterfly,
intrepid as a praying mantis,

wise as a weathered guru,
innocent as yesterday's kitten,

cautious as a Navy Seal,
reckless as a Barbary pirate,

complicated as the Kama Sutra,
simple as the mating of doves,

outrageous as the French Revolution,
studied as the face of the Buddha,

tortured as a Prokoviev concerto,
lyrical as a morning in April,

textured as fresh corduroy,
smooth as mango ice cream,

rapid as the beat of my heart,
slow as the pulse of his love.

Learning to Swim

Afraid to write of my swimming disaster because
he'd think me a sissy and stop loving me,
I decided anyway for truth and not for lies,
not to burrow under metaphor
where anything is everything or nothing.

Yes, I was a disaster at swimming lessons,
summer after summer in Hammond, Indiana.
There was no pool in our Illinois town,
so the Boy Scout mothers took their turns
driving us through the prairie into Indiana.

There I faced the pool once a week
and dreaded it, especially as the boys
around me graduated from the float,
the "dead-man's" float, to the upper end
of the crystal pool, leaving me behind

with the little kids, six years old,
some of whom would kick their way free
to the upper end, leaving me behind,
shame-faced but safe in three feet of water,
trying, trying, trying to float, but unable.

Instructors tried, God knows they tried,
to get me through my fear of water,
but nothing worked, not even when a woman,
sweet from college, lifted the sacred medal
from around my neck, held it up,

and said, "He wouldn't let you drown, would he?"
I shook my brittle head and tried again,
face down in the silver gelatin,
and for one little moment, it worked—I floated.
Then doubt pulled my feet down to the concrete.

I was back where I had started with just
a shred of hope that I'd succeed some day.
It was as if the sun that beat our bones
and hid behind some Indiana cloud
suddenly filled my mind with boyish hope.

It didn't last, of course. I spent the summer
pretending to practice floating. The other boys
never taunted me, never threw
their prowess in my face. I don't know why,
but they left me to my secret dragons.

Eventually I taught myself to swim,
as I did with everything in life,
rarely bound to teachers or their rules.
I don't know when I became a fish or why.
I don't know when I broke away from fear.

Just as I can't remember when I first began
to love you. I'm sure I fought it as I fought
every surge of love for any man,
thinking myself unworthy, or more likely
afraid you'd threaten, jeer and laugh, or run.

I tested the deep end with a poem or two,
then threw myself into the wash of love,
letting myself go, careless of your contact.
Then all at once I realized you'd caught me,
and all my summer fear evaporated.

I swam along your tough iambics, swam
among your Texas metaphors,
swam above your youth and wisdom, swam
below the power of your arms
tightened for the kick and thrust of love.

Now I won't go back to the shallow end
even if you brace your muscle for others.
I've felt your love and won't let go knowing
you are the ballast for my sagging body,
here for me, forever in the water.

In the Second Garden

For I, whose heart's no longer mine,
should you decree it must not live,
will gladly let it die.

—Tasso, 3.27

Here where you take your delight
in the slightest of joys letting
moments of quiet euphoria move
your hours of sorrow off to one side,
where drought is king and the queen
is heaviness, partners in a reign

solidified when your brain
slid down to a conquering night,
reached into the tree, forgetting
injunction, to hell with noise from above
we'd never seen anyway, so we died
in each other and continue the scene

over and over, each touch to mean
we don't regret, safe or afraid,
enough of emptiness and fright,
inside each other, only regretting
now and then the bliss, but knowing love
is best in struggle when one hide

fights the other and the ride
to ecstasy results in red and green,
black and gray, not as when we stayed
forever white, laving in the light
obedience taught, loath of upsetting
an unseen god until we got to prove

that we are god in us, every groove
of skin aching in sex as we never lied,
crossing any troubling mind-ravine
about consequence, knowing if we strayed
from one another then real hell might
sling its jaws and sticky netting

around our souls, all our betting
on an afterlife dissolved away from love
which we'd fought so hard for, tried
to justify by contact vein to vein,
muscle to muscle, erect or laid,
lip on lip, wrong or right.

Bird of Paradise

Never a Fellow matched this Topaz—
And his Emerald Swing—
Dower itself—for Babadilo—
Better—Could I bring?
                    —Emily Dickinson

You spread your yellow wings
to the indulgent sun,
and if you muss my feathers,
I have a tongue of fire.

Because I never tire
of your summer beauty,
look for me in gold and white.
I'll bow—it is my duty.

Your gentle fronds
will block my cruising way.
I'm as tall as you—I'll kneel.
You'll whimper as I pray.

You spread your yellow wings
to the indulgent sun,
and if you muss my feathers,
I'll use my tongue of fire.

Love in the Rain

With rain on the larch and Norway maple come
your gentle eyes braving through the gray storm,
racking bushes, tearing ancient limbs from trees.
Among the broken leaves I see your face

lacing paths around the lake, a trace
of love lost to separation from
whatever joys we birthed outside the norm
set by pert society, its wants, its needs.

Once these fractured elms have turned to seed
I'll come back here knowing that the empty space
will nurture new growth, gone from cold and numb
to warm and strong. We'll have no cause to mourn

the past—it's gone—and from the summer storm
new life, new you, will perk among the trees.
So every time I need to see your face
I'll look among the greenery to come.

His Metamorphosis

He graduates from mirror to giver,
and the applause sinks deep into his ears.
He once expected life to be a downer,
but the angels wouldn't let him sink

into the water of despair—they linked
him to a passing cloud, and so he lives,
a virgin poet oaring boos and cheers
past the smirking devils, past the clowns.

Every effort rows him through the human sounds,
takes him skyward where he tries to drink
the milk of cherubim, but they drink his.
The ache of loss recedes, drifts in fears

that evanesce: he's God now, and he hears
the kiss of grace as it daily pounds
its way into his steel. No need to think
when colors spin and that has turned to this.

Le Jeu est Fait

In life we take what we can get:
the poor a bike, the rich a jet.

The wren that tries to be a dove
ends up in therapy, out of love.

The black who cries that he's not white
becomes a basket-case by night.

The jock who moans he needs a brain
pounds his head and goes insane.

The gay who falls for a straight
succumbs to madness soon or late.

I played my cards and hoped that you
had cards to shuffle, old or new.

I played my hand and saw your eyes
blink once or twice and then grow wise.

I wanted once to be your lover.
I'll settle now to be your brother.

One Year after the Fall

You wanted me to love you so I did,
crossed all the T's and dotted all the I's,
then sealed the contract with a sudden kiss
you never got because I never gave.

I was afraid of you, and so I hid
behind a poetry laced with sighs.
I was afraid you'd go and I would miss
my final opportunity for love.

But you didn't go. I found in you
enough surprise to linger. Caught off guard,
you found my gambit worked—it was enough

to lecture you the way that teachers do
when they can sense a talent in the rough—
I love you when you're hard and when you're soft.

Colossus Down

In his fragility I love him down
among the harbor scraps pulling shards
of broken self from seaweed and detritus,
fighting with sea urchins for his body.

There where the world is ever green and brown
he's landed with a thud broken hard
of crockery. No longer can he fight us
 with a sullen sneer, superior and haughty.

We're equals now—his imperfect lines cracked,
waiting for the glue to harden, mastered
through the fall in time and empty space

to settle chastened in the mud, sacked
by celestial linemen, cruising bastards
who forgot he'd resurrect with grace.

The Truth about Change

You think you live in Texas, but you don't.
You close your eyes and see those country roads,
those dusty, gusty roads, flicking dirt
to ditches where the snakes and rabbits hide,
where flowers wait their turn in seed for spring.

I have walked those roads where everything
endures the summer sun and winter won't
soften the hurt of drought, the gritty modes
of reverie, the reverence of hurt.
A boy on a rusty bike can ride

those paths whipped by weeds side to side
and hope for early love to rise and sing
his charm to lust. But what you learned by rote—
that fish can swim and princes come from toads—
sets off inside your soul a gray alert

that nothing stays, that change and fate subvert
our best intentions, fossil bones have lied
about our permanence, and time will bring
verbena, bluebonnets, your annual hope
finality. But mockingbirds with loads

of summer gilt will spike the prickly goads
of conscience as your sometime joys revert
to neutral colors. Once your body's died
to expectation, your soul is left to wing
not in Texas anymore but in my heart.

Christmas

Yon's the bridegroom, d'ye not spy him?
See how all the ladies eye him.
Venus his perfection findeth,
And no more Adonis mindeth.
Much of him my heart divineth,
On whose brow all virtue shineth.
                              —George Wither

Like the sad dread before the music starts,
when the winter concert hall holds its breath
with an audience filtering in from the cold
of Indiana and whispering "it's time,"

I wait for news from Texas. Then lyric parts
the air, and melody full of birth and death
comes winging from the drowsy stage to hold
me tense against the ache of strings and chime.

Nothing cures the hurt this evening, not
clarinet or oboe, not the brass
or tympani, surely not the flute.

They may as well play silence—what they've got
couldn't heal a heart. I'll take a pass
tonight and think of you, my only truth.

Another Farewell

Is there anything uglier than an empty heart?
I've called your childish name a thousand times
to the wind and let it drop serene among
the unholy few who read these tortured lines.

You can't say I haven't done my part,
parsed among the literati my crimes
and thumbed my nose at taste and even sung
my lyrics to the more than stupefied.

It's over now. My harp's up on the wall
among the bric-à-brac of love and war
to catch a snatch of sunlight now and then.

I'm breathing better here in my caul
of rectitude, kin to saint and whore,
but I could come back—just say when.

What Paul Taught

I didn't know there're boundaries to love,
that you can't love a child or love a man,
that certain daffodils are off our limits
and some orangutans can't be touched.

When I was young I never learned that such
remorseless fences were decreed from above
or that you'd better prefer an apple than
a peach or melon, that lurking criminals

await behind each bush subliminal,
that angels may exist but not for us
to fondle. So I've learned my lessons tough
and memorized the games we play. I can

pass for understated. When I ran
for king I carried a psalter book and hymnal,
kept my heart inside its cavity,
my mind monitoring my captive hands.

Vessel of Clay

*Moses, to prevent anyone from placing God's image
in the flesh of man, first narrates that the body was
formed out of clay, and makes no mention of the
image of God.*
　　　　　　　—Calvin, Psychopannychia

I open the mold before the plaster sets,
release you into the clammy air
letting you be the earthen man
you were supposed to be until
my wanton handling of the clay.

The cast splits wide this morning
letting blue light into darkness.
You breathe the freshness,
and the figure you were meant to be
starts to grow on its own terms.

No thumbs in the mud can turn you
into a vase you were not called to be.
Let your arms flex free, your heart
segue through the fibers of ache,
relax from the heat and sand.

But I will never abandon the kiln.
I remember the waters of adoption running
from your head to your feet to the floor.
Sunlight today bakes you to maturity,
your mighty heart thrilling to its own beat.

Dancing in the Dark

My love for you will never
steady itself like fine rain
in spring or an April sunset.

No, it will always leap like
a calf the hills forgot because
the grass needed their attention.

And as you rise into my conscience,
the will of "yes" asserts
its flowers in a morning dew

where colors matter in a universe
gone black and gray, me here,
you over there with the respectables.

So should I choose a dahlia
over the curve of your smile,
an aster for your touch?

Thank god for memory—
it wades us through the garden
gone to weed and seed

anticipating the buck of winter
who comes demur in white,
leaning in the yard on empty trees.

You can't fade I reminisce,
as the ginger of your hair
throttles all my energy.

And then I rest against your strength,
renewed in amethyst of autumn,
that season of soft light

where you can metamorphose
in a tight cocoon of distance
threaded through and through with love.

A Letter to Gareth

I cannot answer the question of appearances
or that of identity beyond the grave,
But I walk or sit indifferent, I am satisfied,
He ahold of my hand has completely satisfied me.
                    —*Walt Whitman, Calamus*

When I navigated the back streets
of New Jersey's Camden looking
for the cemetery that boasted
Whitman's tomb self-designed,

I never thought that thirty years
later I would be a Whitman too,
but a different Whitman,
not as brazen, more than brazen.

I had already done his house,
the one on Mickle Street,
not the one decaying sadly
on Stevens Street a block away.

I had seen his chair and slippers,
his stuffed parrot, the bed
he died in, his bathing trough,
even his prim outhouse in the back yard.

I had saturated myself in
the living remains of good old Whitman,
even had my photo taken out front,
jauntily, hand on hip like Whitman.

So, filled with the living, I sought out
the dead, found the cemetery,
dreary under a little rain.
I drove the rental car around the paths.

Away from all the other graves,
quiet on the side of a motionless tarn,
the gray granite little house
poked its way up into summer trees.

I parked and went to the tomb-house,
looked in through the iron grate
at shelves of tombs, and there
among the rest rested the Good Gray Poet.

Alone at last with the old gay bard,
I felt as close to him as I'd ever get,
snapped a photo and culled a leaf,
then traced my way back out into Camden.

Whitman loved men, young men,
streetcar conductors and stevedores,
men of the people, men to impel
his solitary exultant verse.

And so I too depend on you,
football player and poet-to-be,
to throw my soul to the clouds
where I have not been in fifteen years.

There I gather my metaphors
and spin them into lines that
celebrate you, beard and shoulders,
eyes and steel-twisted arms.

If you were not singing in my heart,
I would not sing in words,
and the summer would die in a whimper,
bloodless, lacking the verve of juices.

You go on retreat, holying yourself,
somewhere south of the city,
on a ranch where the horses
dissipate the hay and your energy.

I stay behind and count the days,
knowing an hour with you is
Whitman's hour with Peter Doyle,
over and over across the years.

You age like a soldier, from the waist up,
and your ginger hair swims in the wind,
as your heart hungers for meaning
in a world tipping to dissolution.

If I ever gave up on life
it was because you were not here,
a gift to the heat and the drought
of Texas and my heart.

When you pasture your questions
in my cluttered mind, ideas
meld to a firmness and words
find a stallion to ride into meaning.

Now autumn descends, slowly pushing
the summer sun into memory,
bringing cool to my ardor,
hardening it to permanence.

You are part of my being,
a part of the soul we share
now, yesterday, and into the eternity
I wish for, hope against hope.

Frozen

Frozen like Mallarmé facing
the blank sheet of my mind,
anxious to write but afraid
it will not be good enough for you.

The first garden was spontaneous,
fresh and utterly clean.
The second garden was tortured,
imitative, a mind in anxiety.

I want the final garden beatific,
the absolute perfection
of you in me, and I am afraid
to begin, afraid of the page.

Could I trust my muse,
that's you, I would plunge,
let you steer me where
you want the garden to form,

but that would take faith,
supreme hope in your expert hands
at the till of my poem.
I want that, but I am reluctant

to release my power
into capable arms young
for life, fit for direction.
Why do I hesitate? Take me.

In the Final Garden

"O young lord-lover, what sighs are those,
For one that will never be thine?
But mine, but mine," I swore to the rose,
"For ever and ever, mine."
                                    —Tennyson

There where we'll meet naked and the sun
never clouds, content to let the day
wax forever, sweetening what night
would lave us in, rinsed from whatever sin
affection thought improper, among the stars
shining as the eons swirl around

our resurrected bodies bright with sound
of strings and reeds, soft violins and one
calm oboe circling through our hearts, the May
of Januaries swelling on our right,
our orchestrated bliss we find both in
and out each other, when nothing mars

our happiness, no incompleteness jars
our every attitude wrapped around
your chest, my arms, the rapture never done,
enduring long beyond what angels say
eternity is made for, ambered light,
no loss, just you in me, win after win,

the ecstasy of hard completion, tin
for steel, blood for nectar, and the bars
society had screamed gone, the pound
of flesh on flesh a music as we run
our hearts beyond our heads and pray
no prayer because we know our frozen fright

of wonder in our former lives might
have paused us then, but no expected din
of rules will stop our love, no ends, no pars,
no this or that from regulation or mound
of expectation, payment for the fun
of being man with man, a lay

in rapture undisturbed, a South Seas bay
of beauty reconciled to age, the height
at last achieved of wonder, feather from fin,
and certitude, the final longs and fars,
imbuing our souls, locked forever around
each other, not two souls, only one.

Green Pastures

That evening we ate at the old
mansion-restaurant, you stood
under an ancient live-oak tree
and let me take your picture.

A white peacock sat above you
on a green-gray limb,
but the quiet symbol of your
confirmation made no sound.

Almost alone inside a dining room
lined with centuries-old walnut,
we were guarded by a piano
that could have known a pioneer's touch.

Only the next day when I loaded
photos into a computer did I see
that your beard was gone,
and I was shocked at the new face.

To this day I don't understand
why I didn't note the loss
as soon as you jumped in my car
or as you ate in that solemn house.

Hair must be an incidental to be overlooked
when souls have negotiating business
or poetry to bind them heart to heart,
one sonnet flowing to another.

Or maybe the sight of an angel
simply freezes all my senses,
making me incapable of discerning
details like hair and skin and face.

But even now, months later, when
that sweet evening stalks into my brain,
I can remember little else except
you shorn, standing under the white peacock.

Now and Then

I will fight no more forever.
                    —*Chief Joseph*

When I think of you and realize that I'll
take a century to process every
episode of you in me, I dream
of soft eternity outside of time

when minutes will be you as ages fly
unnoticed past my filtering dust and several
angels rearrange my tomb, the scream
of false mortality lost in my grime.

If now I have to lie for hours when you
can settle into me accommodating
life, responsibilities, and new

distractions daily, then there will be few
if any thoughts but you who will be waiting
quietly to king me false or true.

Self Control

I'd seen and touched you,
heard and smelled you,
but I'd yet to taste you

except the sense you'd slipped
into the tongue and stomach
of my hungry soul.

I absorbed you, salt and sugar,
cream and vinegar, knowing
everything you are I could become.

Then the sweet drops slipping down
my agitated throat provoked
my heart to wonder at your ache,

but I accepted every thrust,
reward for my summer
self-denial, the drought my body cried.

Another Gets Away

He watched his arms, and as they opened wide
At every stroke betwixt them would he slide
And steal a kiss, and then run out and dance,
And as he turned, cast many a lustful glance.
                    —*Christopher Marlowe*

I went fishing with a net so fine
I thought no minnow could escape the mesh,
and yet the biggest trout apparently
has slipped into the muck and disappeared.

The water, calm as glass, I hadn't feared,
nor the granite rocks where my line
didn't snag, not once, and my opal flesh
sang the morning sweetly, reverently.

My arms enjoyed the task with a guarantee
of early luck. Suddenly a beard
brushed once against my foot. I thought "he's mine!"
and tugged the swivels shut. What happened next

became a dream of touch and liquid sex.
We wrestled in the slime of river weed.
I slipped, and he swam off a little queered,
experienced, through the logs and vine.

Sestina

Learn from hence, Reader, what small trust
We owe the world, where virtue must,
Frail as our flesh, crumble to dust.
                    —Thomas Carew

I watched him swim away, and the morning,
rarely happy with whatever night
has left it, hardened as the reddening sun
rose higher on the river, and the moon
of my beating heart metered down. A gust
eerily lifted off the water, and a calm

filled me toe to head—as a sutured calm
should after trauma. He had been my morning
week by week. Just like a sweetened gust
he broke into my dreams one wetting night
when my calloused hands maneuvered the moon
off his back and face and chest. Once the sun

discovered where we lay, we found the sun
a friend of sweat and juice before the calm
of cleavage, his and mine. We found the moon
a distant friend as our early morning
muscles probed the crevices that night
ignored. Our conversation was a gust

he could resist but barely, just a gust
he let caress his bearded cheeks when the sun
moved slowly on the river. Deep as night,
our watery explosions dropped to calm
our tightened eyes. Then the gentle morning
laved our legs unclenched, and the moon

dissolved into our hearts, a summer moon
that watched us splash as an early gust
ejected from the rocks, a gift the morning
used to bathe our feet while the smiling sun
amused the minnows swirling in the calm
the eddies left. We had passed from night

to day uncovered, nude, for the night
redeemed us. But the parting time, the moon
had warned us, came with dawn, and the calm
of resurrection wrapped our souls. Like a gust
he pulled away from me, my heart, my sun,
and gave himself to the river's morning.

He washed and left me morning as the night
slipped off his body's sun, and the moon,
my heart, became a gust—he—then calm.

"*Sir Gawayne! leve thy fyghtynge with thy brothir, sir Gareth!*"

And whan he herde hir sey so, he threwe away his shylde and his swerde, and ran to sir Gareth and toke hym in his armys, and sytten kneled downe and asked hym mercy.

Than sir Gareth unlaced hys helme, and kneled downe to hym and asked hym mercy. Than they arose bothe, and braced eythir othir in there armys, and wepte a grete whyle or they myght speke; and eythir of them gaff other the pryse of the batayle, and there were many kynde wordys betwene them.

—*Sir Thomas Malory*